This book belongs to:

Table of Contents

Table of Contents

Table of Contents

Table of Contents

Table of Contents

Table of Contents

Table of Contents

Table of Contents

Recipe ______________________

RECIPE
1

Date: ______________ Prep Time: ______________

Rating: ☆☆☆☆☆ Cook Time: ______________ # of Servings: ______

Ingredients:

Instructions:

NOTES

Recipe ____________________

RECIPE
2

Date: ____________ Prep Time: ____________

Rating: ☆☆☆☆☆ Cook Time: ____________ # of Servings: ______

Ingredients:

Instructions:

NOTES

Recipe ____________________

RECIPE 3

Date: ____________ Prep Time: ____________

Rating: ☆☆☆☆☆ Cook Time: ____________ # of Servings: ______

Ingredients:

Instructions:

NOTES

Recipe

RECIPE
4

Date:

Prep Time:

Rating: ☆☆☆☆☆

Cook Time:

# of Servings:

Ingredients:

Instructions:

NOTES

Recipe ____________________

RECIPE
5

Date: ______________ Prep Time: ______________

Rating: ☆☆☆☆☆ Cook Time: ______________ # of Servings: ______

Ingredients:

Instructions:

NOTES

Recipe ____________________

RECIPE 6

Date: ____________ Prep Time: ____________

Rating: ☆☆☆☆☆ Cook Time: ____________ # of Servings: ________

Ingredients:

Instructions:

NOTES

Recipe ______________________

RECIPE 7

Date: ____________ Prep Time: ____________

Rating: ☆☆☆☆☆ Cook Time: ____________ # of Servings: ______

Ingredients:

Instructions:

NOTES

Recipe ____________________

RECIPE 8

Date: ____________ Prep Time: ____________

Rating: ☆☆☆☆☆ Cook Time: ____________ # of Servings: ________

Ingredients:

Instructions:

NOTES

Recipe ____________________

RECIPE
9

Date: ____________ **Prep Time:** ____________

Rating: ☆☆☆☆☆ **Cook Time:** ____________ **# of Servings:** ________

Ingredients:

Instructions:

NOTES

Recipe

RECIPE 10

Date:

Prep Time:

Rating: ☆☆☆☆☆

Cook Time:

# of Servings:

Ingredients:

Instructions:

NOTES

Recipe ____________________

RECIPE
11

Date: ____________ **Prep Time:** ____________

Rating: ☆☆☆☆☆ **Cook Time:** ____________ **# of Servings:** ______

Ingredients:

Instructions:

NOTES

Recipe ____________________

RECIPE
12

Date: ____________ Prep Time: ____________

Rating: ☆☆☆☆☆ Cook Time: ____________ # of Servings: ________

Ingredients:

Instructions:

NOTES

Recipe ______________________

RECIPE
13

Date: ____________ **Prep Time:** ____________

Rating: ☆☆☆☆☆ **Cook Time:** ____________ **# of Servings:** ______

Ingredients:

Instructions:

NOTES

Recipe ________________

RECIPE
14

Date: ____________ Prep Time: ____________

Rating: ☆☆☆☆☆ Cook Time: ____________ # of Servings: ______

Ingredients:

Instructions:

NOTES

Recipe

RECIPE 15

Date:

Prep Time:

Rating: ☆☆☆☆☆

Cook Time:

# of Servings:

Ingredients:

Instructions:

NOTES

Recipe ____________________

RECIPE 16

Date: ____________ Prep Time: ____________

Rating: ☆☆☆☆☆ Cook Time: ____________ # of Servings: ________

Ingredients:

Instructions:

NOTES

Recipe ______________________

RECIPE
17

Date: ____________ Prep Time: ____________

Rating: ☆☆☆☆☆ Cook Time: ____________ # of Servings: ______

Ingredients:

Instructions:

NOTES

Recipe ______________________

RECIPE
18

Date: ______________ Prep Time: ______________

Rating: ☆☆☆☆☆ Cook Time: ______________ # of Servings: ________

Ingredients:

Instructions:

NOTES

Recipe ______________________

RECIPE
19

Date: ____________ Prep Time: ______________
Rating: ☆☆☆☆☆ Cook Time: ______________ # of Servings: ______

Ingredients:

Instructions:

NOTES

Recipe ______________________

RECIPE 20

Date: ____________ Prep Time: ____________

Rating: ☆☆☆☆☆ Cook Time: ____________ # of Servings: ______

Ingredients:

Instructions:

NOTES

Recipe ___________________________

RECIPE
21

Date: ______________ **Prep Time:** ______________

Rating: ☆☆☆☆☆ **Cook Time:** ______________ **# of Servings:** ________

Ingredients:

Instructions:

NOTES

Recipe ______________________

RECIPE
22

Date: ______________ Prep Time: ______________

Rating: ☆☆☆☆☆ Cook Time: ______________ # of Servings: ________

Ingredients:

Instructions:

NOTES

Recipe ______________________

RECIPE
23

Date: ____________ **Prep Time:** ____________

Rating: ☆☆☆☆☆ **Cook Time:** ____________ **# of Servings:** ______

Ingredients:

Instructions:

NOTES

Recipe ____________________

RECIPE 24

Date: ____________ Prep Time: ____________

Rating: ☆☆☆☆☆ Cook Time: ____________ # of Servings: ________

Ingredients:

Instructions:

NOTES

Recipe ____________________

RECIPE 25

Date: ____________ **Prep Time:** ____________

Rating: ☆☆☆☆☆ **Cook Time:** ____________ **# of Servings:** ________

Ingredients:

Instructions:

NOTES

Recipe

RECIPE
26

Date:

Prep Time:

Rating: ☆☆☆☆☆

Cook Time:

# of Servings:

Ingredients:

Instructions:

NOTES

Recipe ______________________

RECIPE 27

Date: ____________ Prep Time: ____________

Rating: ☆☆☆☆☆ Cook Time: ____________ # of Servings: ______

Ingredients:

Instructions:

NOTES

Recipe ______________________

RECIPE
28

Date: ______________ **Prep Time:** ______________

Rating: ☆☆☆☆☆ **Cook Time:** ______________ **# of Servings:** ________

Ingredients:

Instructions:

NOTES

Recipe

RECIPE 29

Date:

Prep Time:

Rating: ☆☆☆☆☆

Cook Time:

# of Servings:

Ingredients:

Instructions:

NOTES

Recipe ____________________

RECIPE
30

Date: ____________ Prep Time: ____________

Rating: ☆☆☆☆☆ Cook Time: ____________ # of Servings: ________

Ingredients:

Instructions:

NOTES

Recipe

RECIPE
31

Date:

Prep Time:

Rating: ☆☆☆☆☆

Cook Time:

# of Servings:

Ingredients:

Instructions:

NOTES

Recipe ______________________

RECIPE
32

Date: ____________ **Prep Time:** ____________

Rating: ☆☆☆☆☆ **Cook Time:** ____________ **# of Servings:** ______

Ingredients:

Instructions:

NOTES

Recipe ________________________

RECIPE
33

Date: ____________ Prep Time: ____________

Rating: ☆☆☆☆☆ Cook Time: ____________ # of Servings: ______

Ingredients:

Instructions:

NOTES

Recipe ___

RECIPE 34

Date: ___ Prep Time: ___

Rating: ☆☆☆☆☆ Cook Time: ___ # of Servings: ___

Ingredients:

Instructions:

NOTES

Recipe ______________________

RECIPE
35

Date: ______________ **Prep Time:** ______________

Rating: ☆☆☆☆☆ **Cook Time:** ______________ **# of Servings:** ________

Ingredients:

Instructions:

NOTES

Recipe ______________________

RECIPE
36

Date: ______________ Prep Time: ______________

Rating: ☆☆☆☆☆ Cook Time: ______________ # of Servings: ________

Ingredients:

Instructions:

NOTES

Recipe

RECIPE
37

Date:

Prep Time:

Rating: ☆☆☆☆☆

Cook Time:

# of Servings:

Ingredients:

Instructions:

NOTES

Recipe

RECIPE 38

Date:

Prep Time:

Rating: ☆☆☆☆☆

Cook Time:

# of Servings:

Ingredients:

Instructions:

NOTES

Recipe

RECIPE
39

Date:
Prep Time:
Rating: ☆☆☆☆☆
Cook Time:
# of Servings:

Ingredients:

Instructions:

NOTES

Recipe ______________________

RECIPE 40

Date: ______________ Prep Time: ______________

Rating: ☆☆☆☆☆ Cook Time: ______________ # of Servings: ________

Ingredients:

Instructions:

NOTES

Recipe ______________________________

RECIPE 41

Date: ______________ Prep Time: ______________

Rating: ☆☆☆☆☆ Cook Time: ______________ # of Servings: ______

Ingredients:

Instructions:

NOTES

Recipe ______________________

RECIPE
42

Date: ______________ **Prep Time:** ______________

Rating: ☆☆☆☆☆ **Cook Time:** ______________ **# of Servings:** ______

Ingredients:

Instructions:

NOTES

Recipe ____________________

RECIPE 43

Date: ____________ Prep Time: ____________

Rating: ☆☆☆☆☆ Cook Time: ____________ # of Servings: ________

Ingredients:

Instructions:

NOTES

Recipe

RECIPE 44

Date:

Prep Time:

Rating: ☆☆☆☆☆

Cook Time:

# of Servings:

Ingredients:

Instructions:

NOTES

Recipe

RECIPE 45

Date: ______ **Prep Time:** ______

Rating: ☆☆☆☆☆ **Cook Time:** ______ **# of Servings:** ______

Ingredients:

Instructions:

NOTES

Recipe ____________________

RECIPE
46

Date: ____________ Prep Time: ____________

Rating: ☆☆☆☆☆ Cook Time: ____________ # of Servings: ______

Ingredients:

Instructions:

NOTES

Recipe ______________________

RECIPE
47

Date: ____________ Prep Time: ____________

Rating: ☆☆☆☆☆ Cook Time: ____________ # of Servings: ________

Ingredients:

Instructions:

NOTES

Recipe ______________________

RECIPE
48

Date: ____________ **Prep Time:** ____________

Rating: ☆☆☆☆☆ **Cook Time:** ____________ **# of Servings:** ________

Ingredients:

Instructions:

NOTES

Recipe

RECIPE 49

Date:

Prep Time:

Rating: ☆☆☆☆☆

Cook Time:

# of Servings:

Ingredients:

Instructions:

NOTES

Recipe

RECIPE
50

Date:

Prep Time:

Rating: ☆☆☆☆☆

Cook Time:

# of Servings:

Ingredients:

Instructions:

NOTES

Recipe

RECIPE
51

Date:

Prep Time:

Rating: ☆☆☆☆☆

Cook Time:

# of Servings:

Ingredients:

Instructions:

NOTES

Recipe ______________________

RECIPE
52

Date: ____________ **Prep Time:** ____________

Rating: ☆☆☆☆☆ **Cook Time:** ____________ **# of Servings:** ________

Ingredients:

Instructions:

NOTES

Recipe

RECIPE 53

Date:

Prep Time:

Rating: ☆☆☆☆☆

Cook Time:

# of Servings:

Ingredients:

Instructions:

NOTES

Recipe

RECIPE
54

Date:

Prep Time:

Rating: ☆☆☆☆☆

Cook Time:

# of Servings:

Ingredients:

Instructions:

NOTES

Recipe ____________________

RECIPE 55

Date: ____________ Prep Time: ____________

Rating: ☆☆☆☆☆ Cook Time: ____________ # of Servings: ________

Ingredients:

Instructions:

NOTES

Recipe

RECIPE 56

Date:

Prep Time:

Rating: ☆☆☆☆☆

Cook Time:

# of Servings:

Ingredients:

Instructions:

NOTES

Recipe ____________________

RECIPE 57

Date: ______________ **Prep Time:** ______________

Rating: ☆☆☆☆☆ **Cook Time:** ______________ **# of Servings:** ______

Ingredients:

Instructions:

NOTES

Recipe ____________________

RECIPE
58

Date: ____________ Prep Time: ____________

Rating: ☆☆☆☆☆ Cook Time: ____________ # of Servings: ________

Ingredients:

Instructions:

NOTES

Recipe ____________

RECIPE 59

Date: ____________ Prep Time: ____________

Rating: ☆☆☆☆☆ Cook Time: ____________ # of Servings: ______

Ingredients:

Instructions:

NOTES

Recipe

RECIPE 60

Date:

Prep Time:

Rating: ☆☆☆☆☆

Cook Time:

# of Servings:

Ingredients:

Instructions:

NOTES

Recipe

RECIPE 61

Date:

Prep Time:

Rating: ☆☆☆☆☆

Cook Time:

# of Servings:

Ingredients:

Instructions:

NOTES

Recipe ____________________

RECIPE 62

Date: ______________ Prep Time: ______________

Rating: ☆☆☆☆☆ Cook Time: ______________ # of Servings: ________

Ingredients:

Instructions:

NOTES

Recipe

RECIPE
63

Date:

Prep Time:

Rating: ☆☆☆☆☆

Cook Time:

# of Servings:

Ingredients:

Instructions:

NOTES

Recipe ______________________

RECIPE
64

Date: ____________ Prep Time: ____________

Rating: ☆☆☆☆☆ Cook Time: ____________ # of Servings: ________

Ingredients:

Instructions:

NOTES

Recipe ______________________

RECIPE
65

Date: ____________ **Prep Time:** ____________

Rating: ☆☆☆☆☆ **Cook Time:** ____________ **# of Servings:** ________

Ingredients:

Instructions:

NOTES

Recipe

RECIPE
66

Date:

Prep Time:

Rating: ☆☆☆☆☆

Cook Time:

# of Servings:

Ingredients:

Instructions:

NOTES

Recipe ______________________

RECIPE 67

Date: ______________ Prep Time: ______________

Rating: ☆☆☆☆☆ Cook Time: ______________ # of Servings: ________

Ingredients:

Instructions:

NOTES

Recipe ________________________________

RECIPE 68

Date: ________________ Prep Time: ________________

Rating: ☆☆☆☆☆ Cook Time: ________________ # of Servings: ________

Ingredients:

Instructions:

NOTES

Recipe

RECIPE 69

Date:

Prep Time:

Rating: ☆☆☆☆☆

Cook Time:

# of Servings:

Ingredients:

Instructions:

NOTES

Recipe ________________

RECIPE 70

Date: ____________ Prep Time: ____________

Rating: ☆☆☆☆☆ Cook Time: ____________ # of Servings: ______

Ingredients:

Instructions:

NOTES

Recipe ____________________

RECIPE
71

Date: ____________ Prep Time: ____________

Rating: ☆☆☆☆☆ Cook Time: ____________ # of Servings: ______

Ingredients:

Instructions:

NOTES

Recipe ____________________

RECIPE
72

Date: ________ **Prep Time:** ________

Rating: ☆☆☆☆☆ **Cook Time:** ________ **# of Servings:** ________

Ingredients:

Instructions:

NOTES

Recipe

RECIPE 73

Date:

Prep Time:

Rating: ☆☆☆☆☆

Cook Time:

# of Servings:

Ingredients:

Instructions:

NOTES

Recipe ______________________

RECIPE
74

Date: ______________ **Prep Time:** ______________

Rating: ☆☆☆☆☆ **Cook Time:** ______________ **# of Servings:** ________

Ingredients:

Instructions:

NOTES

Recipe

RECIPE 75

Date:

Prep Time:

Rating: ☆☆☆☆☆

Cook Time:

# of Servings:

Ingredients:

Instructions:

NOTES

Recipe

RECIPE 76

Date:

Prep Time:

Rating: ☆☆☆☆☆

Cook Time:

# of Servings:

Ingredients:

Instructions:

NOTES

Recipe ______________________

RECIPE 77

Date: ____________ Prep Time: ____________

Rating: ☆☆☆☆☆ Cook Time: ____________ # of Servings: ______

Ingredients:

Instructions:

NOTES

Recipe ______________________

RECIPE
78

Date: ____________ Prep Time: ____________

Rating: ☆☆☆☆☆ Cook Time: ____________ # of Servings: ________

Ingredients:

Instructions:

NOTES

Recipe ______________________

RECIPE
79

Date: ________ **Prep Time:** ________

Rating: ☆☆☆☆☆ **Cook Time:** ________ **# of Servings:** ________

Ingredients:

Instructions:

NOTES

Recipe

RECIPE 80

Date:

Rating: ☆☆☆☆☆

Prep Time:

Cook Time:

# of Servings:

Ingredients:

Instructions:

NOTES

Recipe ____________________

RECIPE 81

Date: ____________ **Prep Time:** ____________

Rating: ☆☆☆☆☆ **Cook Time:** ____________ **# of Servings:** ______

Ingredients:

Instructions:

NOTES

Recipe

RECIPE
82

Date:
Rating: ☆☆☆☆☆

Prep Time:
Cook Time:

# of Servings:

Ingredients:

Instructions:

NOTES

Recipe ______________________

RECIPE
83

Date: ______________ **Prep Time:** ______________

Rating: ☆☆☆☆☆ **Cook Time:** ______________ **# of Servings:** ________

Ingredients:

Instructions:

NOTES

Recipe ____________________

RECIPE 84

Date: ____________ **Prep Time:** ____________

Rating: ☆☆☆☆☆ **Cook Time:** ____________ **# of Servings:** ______

Ingredients:

Instructions:

NOTES

Recipe ______________________

RECIPE
85

Date: ______________ Prep Time: ______________

Rating: ☆☆☆☆☆ Cook Time: ______________ # of Servings: ______

Ingredients:

Instructions:

NOTES

Recipe

RECIPE
86

Date:

Prep Time:

Rating: ☆☆☆☆☆

Cook Time:

# of Servings:

Ingredients:

Instructions:

NOTES

Recipe ______________________

RECIPE 87

Date: ____________ **Prep Time:** ____________

Rating: ☆☆☆☆☆ **Cook Time:** ____________ **# of Servings:** ______

Ingredients:

Instructions:

NOTES

Recipe ____________________

RECIPE
88

Date: ________ **Prep Time:** ________

Rating: ☆☆☆☆☆ **Cook Time:** ________ **# of Servings:** ________

Ingredients:

Instructions:

NOTES

Recipe ______________________

RECIPE
89

Date: ______________ **Prep Time:** ______________

Rating: ☆☆☆☆☆ **Cook Time:** ______________ **# of Servings:** ______

Ingredients:

Instructions:

NOTES

Recipe ____________________

RECIPE 90

Date: ____________ Prep Time: ____________

Rating: ☆☆☆☆☆ Cook Time: ____________ # of Servings: ________

Ingredients:

Instructions:

NOTES

Recipe ______________________

RECIPE 91

Date: ____________ **Prep Time:** ____________

Rating: ☆☆☆☆☆ **Cook Time:** ____________ **# of Servings:** ______

Ingredients:

Instructions:

NOTES

Recipe ____________________

RECIPE
92

Date: ____________ **Prep Time:** ____________

Rating: ☆☆☆☆☆ **Cook Time:** ____________ **# of Servings:** ______

Ingredients:

Instructions:

NOTES

Recipe ________________

RECIPE 93

Date: ____________ Prep Time: ____________

Rating: ☆☆☆☆☆ Cook Time: ____________ # of Servings: ______

Ingredients:

Instructions:

NOTES

Recipe ____________________

RECIPE 94

Date: ______________ Prep Time: ______________

Rating: ☆☆☆☆☆ Cook Time: ______________ # of Servings: ________

Ingredients:

Instructions:

NOTES

Recipe ______________________

RECIPE
95

Date: ______________ **Prep Time:** ______________

Rating: ☆☆☆☆☆ **Cook Time:** ______________ **# of Servings:** ______

Ingredients:

Instructions:

NOTES

Recipe ___________________

RECIPE 96

Date: ____________ Prep Time: ____________

Rating: ☆☆☆☆☆ Cook Time: ____________ # of Servings: ______

Ingredients:

Instructions:

NOTES

Recipe ____________________

RECIPE 97

Date: __________ **Prep Time:** __________

Rating: ☆☆☆☆☆ **Cook Time:** __________ **# of Servings:** ______

Ingredients:

Instructions:

NOTES

Recipe ____________________

RECIPE
98

Date: ____________ Prep Time: ____________

Rating: ☆☆☆☆☆ Cook Time: ____________ # of Servings: ______

Ingredients:

Instructions:

NOTES

Recipe ______________________

RECIPE 99

Date: ____________ Prep Time: ____________

Rating: ☆☆☆☆☆ Cook Time: ____________ # of Servings: ______

Ingredients:

Instructions:

NOTES

Recipe ____________________

RECIPE
100

Date: ____________ **Prep Time:** ____________

Rating: ☆☆☆☆☆ **Cook Time:** ____________ **# of Servings:** ______

Ingredients:

Instructions:

NOTES

Recipe ______________________

RECIPE 101

Date: ____________ **Prep Time:** ____________

Rating: ☆☆☆☆☆ **Cook Time:** ____________ **# of Servings:** ________

Ingredients:

Instructions:

NOTES

Recipe

RECIPE 102

Date:

Prep Time:

Rating: ☆☆☆☆☆

Cook Time:

# of Servings:

Ingredients:

Instructions:

NOTES

Recipe ______________________

RECIPE 103

Date: ____________ Prep Time: ____________

Rating: ☆☆☆☆☆ Cook Time: ____________ # of Servings: ______

Ingredients:

Instructions:

NOTES

Recipe ____________________

RECIPE 104

Date: ____________ **Prep Time:** ____________

Rating: ☆☆☆☆☆ **Cook Time:** ____________ **# of Servings:** ______

Ingredients:

Instructions:

NOTES

Recipe ____________________

RECIPE 105

Date: ____________ Prep Time: ____________

Rating: ☆☆☆☆☆ Cook Time: ____________ # of Servings: ________

Ingredients:

Instructions:

NOTES

Recipe ______________________

RECIPE
106

Date: ____________ Prep Time: ____________

Rating: ☆☆☆☆☆ Cook Time: ____________ # of Servings: ______

Ingredients:

Instructions:

NOTES

Recipe ___________________________

RECIPE
107

Date: ______________ **Prep Time:** ______________

Rating: ☆☆☆☆☆ **Cook Time:** ______________ **# of Servings:** ______

Ingredients:

Instructions:

NOTES

Recipe ____________________

RECIPE
108

Date: ____________ Prep Time: ____________

Rating: ☆☆☆☆☆ Cook Time: ____________ # of Servings: ______

Ingredients:

Instructions:

NOTES

Recipe ______________________

RECIPE 109

Date: ____________ Prep Time: ____________

Rating: ☆☆☆☆☆ Cook Time: ____________ # of Servings: ______

Ingredients:

Instructions:

NOTES

Recipe ______________________

RECIPE
110

Date: ____________ **Prep Time:** ____________

Rating: ☆☆☆☆☆ **Cook Time:** ____________ **# of Servings:** ________

Ingredients:

Instructions:

NOTES

Recipe

RECIPE 111

Date:

Prep Time:

Rating: ☆☆☆☆☆

Cook Time:

# of Servings:

Ingredients:

Instructions:

NOTES

Recipe

RECIPE 112

Date:

Prep Time:

Rating: ☆☆☆☆☆

Cook Time:

# of Servings:

Ingredients:

Instructions:

NOTES

Recipe

RECIPE 113

Date:

Prep Time:

Rating: ☆☆☆☆☆

Cook Time:

# of Servings:

Ingredients:

Instructions:

NOTES

Recipe ____________________

RECIPE
114

Date: __________ **Prep Time:** __________

Rating: ☆☆☆☆☆ **Cook Time:** __________ **# of Servings:** ______

Ingredients:

Instructions:

NOTES

Recipe ______________________

RECIPE
115

Date: ____________ **Prep Time:** ____________

Rating: ☆☆☆☆☆ **Cook Time:** ____________ **# of Servings:** ______

Ingredients:

Instructions:

NOTES

Recipe ____________________

RECIPE
116

Date: ____________ **Prep Time:** ____________

Rating: ☆☆☆☆☆ **Cook Time:** ____________ **# of Servings:** ______

Ingredients:

Instructions:

NOTES

Recipe ______________________

RECIPE
117

Date: ____________ **Prep Time:** ____________

Rating: ☆☆☆☆☆ **Cook Time:** ____________ **# of Servings:** ________

Ingredients:

Instructions:

NOTES

Recipe ____________________

RECIPE
118

Date: ____________ Prep Time: ____________

Rating: ☆☆☆☆☆ Cook Time: ____________ # of Servings: ______

Ingredients:

Instructions:

NOTES

Recipe ____________________

RECIPE 119

Date: ____________ Prep Time: ____________

Rating: ☆☆☆☆☆ Cook Time: ____________ # of Servings: ______

Ingredients:

Instructions:

NOTES

Recipe ______________________

RECIPE 120

Date: ______________ **Prep Time:** ______________

Rating: ☆☆☆☆☆ **Cook Time:** ______________ **# of Servings:** ______

Ingredients:

Instructions:

NOTES

Recipe ____________________

RECIPE
121

Date: ____________ **Prep Time:** ____________

Rating: ☆☆☆☆☆ **Cook Time:** ____________ **# of Servings:** ________

Ingredients:

Instructions:

NOTES

Recipe

RECIPE 122

Date:

Prep Time:

Rating: ☆☆☆☆☆

Cook Time:

# of Servings:

Ingredients:

Instructions:

NOTES

Recipe ______________________

RECIPE 123

Date: ______________ Prep Time: ______________

Rating: ☆☆☆☆☆ Cook Time: ______________ # of Servings: ________

Ingredients:

Instructions:

NOTES

Recipe ______________________

RECIPE
124

Date: ____________ **Prep Time:** ____________

Rating: ☆☆☆☆☆ **Cook Time:** ____________ **# of Servings:** ______

Ingredients:

Instructions:

NOTES

Recipe ______________________

RECIPE
125

Date: ________ **Prep Time:** ________

Rating: ☆☆☆☆☆ **Cook Time:** ________ **# of Servings:** ________

Ingredients:

Instructions:

NOTES

Recipe ____________________

RECIPE
126

Date: ______________ **Prep Time:** ______________

Rating: ☆☆☆☆☆ **Cook Time:** ______________ **# of Servings:** ________

Ingredients:

Instructions:

NOTES

Recipe ______________________

RECIPE
127

Date: ____________ Prep Time: ____________

Rating: ☆☆☆☆☆ Cook Time: ____________ # of Servings: ______

Ingredients:

Instructions:

NOTES

Recipe ______________________

RECIPE
128

Date: ______________ Prep Time: ______________

Rating: ☆☆☆☆☆ Cook Time: ______________ # of Servings: ______

Ingredients:

Instructions:

NOTES

Recipe ______________________

RECIPE 129

Date: ______________ **Prep Time:** ______________

Rating: ☆☆☆☆☆ **Cook Time:** ______________ **# of Servings:** ________

Ingredients:

Instructions:

NOTES

Recipe ______________________

RECIPE
130

Date: ______________ Prep Time: ______________

Rating: ☆☆☆☆☆ Cook Time: ______________ # of Servings: ______

Ingredients:

Instructions:

NOTES

Recipe ______________________

RECIPE
131

Date: ______________ **Prep Time:** ______________

Rating: ☆☆☆☆☆ **Cook Time:** ______________ **# of Servings:** ______

Ingredients:

Instructions:

NOTES

Recipe

RECIPE 132

Date:

Prep Time:

Rating: ☆☆☆☆☆

Cook Time:

# of Servings:

Ingredients:

Instructions:

NOTES

Recipe

RECIPE 133

Date:

Prep Time:

Rating: ☆☆☆☆☆

Cook Time:

# of Servings:

Ingredients:

Instructions:

NOTES

Recipe ____________________

RECIPE
134

Date: ____________ Prep Time: ____________

Rating: ☆☆☆☆☆ Cook Time: ____________ # of Servings: ________

Ingredients:

Instructions:

NOTES

Recipe ____________________

RECIPE
135

Date: ____________ **Prep Time:** ____________

Rating: ☆☆☆☆☆ **Cook Time:** ____________ **# of Servings:** ______

Ingredients:

Instructions:

NOTES

Recipe ______________________

RECIPE
136

Date: ____________ **Prep Time:** ____________

Rating: ☆☆☆☆☆ **Cook Time:** ____________ **# of Servings:** ______

Ingredients:

Instructions:

NOTES

Recipe ____________________

RECIPE
137

Date: ____________ **Prep Time:** ____________

Rating: ☆☆☆☆☆ **Cook Time:** ____________ **# of Servings:** ______

Ingredients:

Instructions:

NOTES

Recipe

RECIPE 138

Date:

Prep Time:

Rating: ☆☆☆☆☆

Cook Time:

# of Servings:

Ingredients:

Instructions:

NOTES

Recipe ______________________

RECIPE 139

Date: ____________ **Prep Time:** ____________

Rating: ☆☆☆☆☆ **Cook Time:** ____________ **# of Servings:** ______

Ingredients:

Instructions:

NOTES

Recipe ____________________

RECIPE
140

Date: ______________ **Prep Time:** ______________

Rating: ☆☆☆☆☆ **Cook Time:** ______________ **# of Servings:** ________

Ingredients:

Instructions:

NOTES

Recipe ____________________

RECIPE
141

Date: ____________ Prep Time: ____________

Rating: ☆☆☆☆☆ Cook Time: ____________ # of Servings: ______

Ingredients:

Instructions:

NOTES

Recipe ____________________

RECIPE 142

Date: ____________ **Prep Time:** ____________

Rating: ☆☆☆☆☆ **Cook Time:** ____________ **# of Servings:** ______

Ingredients:

Instructions:

NOTES

Recipe ________________

RECIPE 143

Date: ________ Prep Time: ________

Rating: ☆☆☆☆☆ Cook Time: ________ # of Servings: ________

Ingredients:

Instructions:

NOTES

Recipe ____________________

RECIPE
144

Date: ____________ **Prep Time:** ____________

Rating: ☆☆☆☆☆ **Cook Time:** ____________ **# of Servings:** ______

Ingredients:

Instructions:

NOTES

Recipe

RECIPE
145

Date: ____ **Prep Time:** ____

Rating: ☆☆☆☆☆ **Cook Time:** ____ **# of Servings:** ____

Ingredients:

Instructions:

NOTES

Recipe ______________________

RECIPE
146

Date: ____________ **Prep Time:** ____________

Rating: ☆☆☆☆☆ **Cook Time:** ____________ **# of Servings:** ______

Ingredients:

Instructions:

NOTES

Recipe

RECIPE 147

Date:

Prep Time:

Rating: ☆☆☆☆☆

Cook Time:

# of Servings:

Ingredients:

Instructions:

NOTES

Recipe ______________________

RECIPE 148

Date: ____________ **Prep Time:** ____________

Rating: ☆☆☆☆☆ **Cook Time:** ____________ **# of Servings:** ______

Ingredients:

Instructions:

NOTES

Recipe ____________________

RECIPE
149

Date: ____________ Prep Time: ____________

Rating: ☆☆☆☆☆ Cook Time: ____________ # of Servings: ________

Ingredients:

Instructions:

NOTES

Recipe ______________________

RECIPE 150

Date: ______________ Prep Time: ______________

Rating: ☆☆☆☆☆ Cook Time: ______________ # of Servings: ______

Ingredients:

Instructions:

NOTES

Recipe ______________________

RECIPE
151

Date: ______________ **Prep Time:** ______________

Rating: ☆☆☆☆☆ **Cook Time:** ______________ **# of Servings:** ________

Ingredients:

Instructions:

NOTES

Recipe ____________________

RECIPE
152

Date: ____________ Prep Time: ____________

Rating: ☆☆☆☆☆ Cook Time: ____________ # of Servings: ______

Ingredients:

Instructions:

NOTES

Recipe ______________________

RECIPE
153

Date: ____________ **Prep Time:** ____________

Rating: ☆☆☆☆☆ **Cook Time:** ____________ **# of Servings:** ________

Ingredients:

Instructions:

NOTES

Recipe ______________________

RECIPE
154

Date: ______________ Prep Time: ______________

Rating: ☆☆☆☆☆ Cook Time: ______________ # of Servings: ________

Ingredients:

Instructions:

NOTES

Recipe ____________________

RECIPE
155

Date: ________ **Prep Time:** ________

Rating: ☆☆☆☆☆ **Cook Time:** ________ **# of Servings:** ________

Ingredients:

Instructions:

NOTES

Recipe ____________________

RECIPE
156

Date: ______________ **Prep Time:** ______________

Rating: ☆☆☆☆☆ **Cook Time:** ______________ **# of Servings:** ________

Ingredients:

Instructions:

NOTES

Recipe ______________________

RECIPE 157

Date: ____________ Prep Time: ____________

Rating: ☆☆☆☆☆ Cook Time: ____________ # of Servings: ______

Ingredients:

Instructions:

NOTES

Recipe ______________________

RECIPE
158

Date: ____________ Prep Time: ____________

Rating: ☆☆☆☆☆ Cook Time: ____________ # of Servings: ______

Ingredients:

Instructions:

NOTES

Recipe ______________________

RECIPE 159

Date: ____________ Prep Time: ____________

Rating: ☆☆☆☆☆ Cook Time: ____________ # of Servings: ______

Ingredients:

Instructions:

NOTES

Recipe ______________________

RECIPE
160

Date: ____________ **Prep Time:** ____________

Rating: ☆☆☆☆☆ **Cook Time:** ____________ **# of Servings:** ______

Ingredients:

Instructions:

NOTES

Made in the USA
Middletown, DE
03 December 2024

66084636R00095